Wishing you many happy date nights!
Shelley Marsh

Fifty
First Coast Dates

Shelley D. Marsh

Palm Valley Press
Ponte Vedra Beach, Florida

Copyright © 2013 by ShelleyMarsh.

All rights reserved. No part of this publication may be reproduced, distributed or transmitted in any form or by any means, including photocopying, recording, or other electronic or mechanical methods, without the prior written permission of the publisher, except in the case of brief quotations embodied in critical reviews and certain other noncommercial uses permitted by copyright law. For permission requests, write to the publisher, addressed "Attention: Permissions Coordinator," at the address below.

Palm Valley Press
3787 Palm Valley Road Suite 102-105
Ponte Vedra Beach, Florida 32082
www.fiftyfundates.com

Book Layout ©2013 BookDesignTemplates.com

Ordering Information:
Quantity sales. Special discounts are available on quantity purchases by corporations, associations, and others. For details, contact the "Special Sales Department" at the address above.

Fifty First Coast Dates/ Shelley Marsh. —1st ed.
ISBN 978-0-9899225-2-4

Contents

Introduction	6
Art Museums & Galleries	9
Art Gallery Opening	10
Art Walk	10
Theater and Music	12
Florida Theater	12
Times-Union Center for the Performing Arts	13
Saint Augustine Amphitheatre	14
Museums and History	15
Museum of Science and History	15
St Augustine Pirate and Treasure museum	16
Ripley's Odditorium	17
Gentleman's Choice	19
Professional Sporting Events	19
Pool Hall	21
Gun Play	22
Old School	25
Arcade Night	25
"Fore!" Play	26

Dune Buggy Rides	27
Roller Skating	27
Bowling	28
Back to Nature	**31**
Picnic in the park	31
A Walk on the Beach	32
Paddling (kayaks and Canoes, that is)	33
Mood Music	**35**
Concerts al Fresco (and all free-o)	35
Jazz it up	37
Springing the Blues	38
Dance Club	39
Nothin but Mammals	**41**
Horseback Ride on the Beach	42
Eat, Drink and Be Merry	**44**
Spice up your relationship with exotic food	44
Waterfront Dining	49
Fondue for Two	51
Taste the First Coast	52
Wine Tasting	53
Comedy Club	54

Scarlett and Rhett's	55
Cuban Food and Dancing	56
Dinner and a Movie	**58**
Cinema Grill	58
Moonlight Movies	59
Learning Together	**61**
Cooking for Two	61
Martial Arts	62
Parallel Painting	63
Board? (surfboard, that is) Take a lesson!	64
Dance Lesson	66
Tour the Town	**69**
River Cruises	69
Carriage Tours	70
Ghostly Outings	71
Brewery Tours and Tastings	72
Cycling	74
Nights of Lights	75
Wrap it Up	**77**
Couples Massage	77
Conclusion	**79**

*To Robert, my partner on the roadtrip of life,
and
To Mama, my constant encourager and free babysitter.*

Introduction

In even the healthiest relationships, boredom can set in. The daily routines of work, household duties, and in some cases child rearing can lead to fatigue and inertia. Many couples give up on having a regularly scheduled date night. If children are involved, the expense of a babysitter often makes a night out prohibitively expensive.

Carving out regularly scheduled opportunities for one-on-one time is crucial to maintaining a healthy relationship. *The Marriage Project* is a long-term study conducted at the University of Virginia by W. Bradford Wilcox and Jeffrey Dew. They found that date nights can be "instrumental for cultivating and maintaining an intense emotional or romantic connection with one another." Furthermore, they found that couples who spend time together at least once a week were 3.5 times more likely to describe themselves as happy in their relationship. (*The National Marriage Project, 2012*) Psychologist and author Dr. Tammy Nelson proposes that "regular date nights are important for marriages" ("Date Nights: They Make Your Marriage Work," Huffington Post, 2012). An article in The Inquisitr asserts "that partners who devote one date or more a week to date nights have a higher level of communication, better sex lives and a stronger commitment to one another compared to non-date night participating married couples. (*Date Nights Improve Marriage, Better Your Sex Life,* by James Johnson).

While money has been an obstacle to many couples who would like to go out with their spouse, a recent article in the Washington Post found that coupon programs such as Groupon, Living Social and others have lessened the financial impediment to date night. (*Washington*

Post, Steve Hendrix, February 2012). Many ideas you will find in this book require little or no money (see "Concerts Al Fresco," "A Walk on the Beach" and "Wine Tastings").

Don't assume that all the couples who might utilize the ideas in this book are all married. On the contrary, even single guys can benefit from a little inspiration when it comes to creative dating. "Date Number Two" is much more likely to happen when "Date Number One" was exciting and fun.

Fifty Fun First Coast Dates is certain to become a valuable resource for users who find themselves asking, "What do you want to do tonight?" Keep it in the car for reference when on the go, or use it for planning ahead. Take turns with his and her selections weekly, or randomly turn to a page and go wherever your finger lands. Any way you choose to use it, *Fifty First Dates* will help liven up your next date night.

[1]
Art Museums & Galleries

"Sometimes you have to let art flow over you.".
—The Big Chill, 1983

LOCAL ART MUSEUMS offer extended hours on selected evenings, providing a perfect opportunity for an artful date night.

The Cummer Museum in the Riverside neighborhood leaves the lights on until 9 pm each Tuesday night. As an added benefit, admission is free after 4pm. The museum houses a permanent collection of over 5000 pieces, as well as traveling exhibits from around the world. The gardens behind the museum feature a beautiful view of the river as well as many romantic nooks where a couple might sit and enjoy the sunset or the stars. Suggested romantic restaurant pairing: Black Sheep Restaurant

The Cummer Museum of Art and Gardens, (904) 356-6857

829 Riverside Avenue, Jacksonville Florida 32204
www.cummer.org

If modern art is more your speed, the Museum of Contemporary Art, or MOCA, is open until 8 pm on Thursday nights. Evenings at the MOCA often feature special film presentations or lectures. Café

NOLA is open for dinner, and features upscale dining in a unique setting. The menu is described as Mediterranean with Southern influences. Call for reservations.

Museum of Contemporary Art (904) 366-6911

333 N Laura Street, Jacksonville Florida 32202

www.mocajacksonville.org

Art Gallery Opening

Many galleries feature opening nights events for new exhibitions. These events are often free to the public and frequently feature hors d'oeuvres and drinks. Peruse the collection & make astute comments to impress your date.

Art Walk

If you'd like to be free to roam instead of confining your art appreciation to one museum, try one of the many local art walks offered on various evenings each month.

The first Wednesday of every month is ArtWalk in downtown Jacksonville. This event takes place, rain or shine, from 5 to 9pm. Local galleries, museums, and restaurants participate, and a different theme is featured each month. Art Walk Jacksonville is a self-guided walking tour, and maps are available for download on the website.

North Beaches ArtWalk hosts an event every third Thursday from 5 to 9, rain or shine. Located at the Beaches Town Center, North Beaches ArtWalk is "the best little art walk in town." Local artists display their work on tables along covered walkways. Nearby restaurants offer specials during the event: Starbucks gives out free samples, and Al's Pizza offers $1 wine and drafts. Maps are available online.

The art galleries of Saint Augustine are open late for First Friday ArtWalk, the first Friday of each month. This event is also self-guided, and maps are available online or at any participating gallery. Park at any of the participating AGOSA galleries or take advantage of the free Artwalk Trolley, starting at 6pm on King Street. You can also park at San Sebastian Winery or Rembrantz to catch the trolley, which makes a loop of all the galleries. The trolley might be advisable if you plan to enjoy many free wine samples.

In Fernandina Beach, the second Saturday of every month marks their Artrageous Artwalk from 5:30 to 8:30. Twelve local galleries participate in this event, most located on Centre Street. Many restaurants and bars are also located along this quaint, cobblestone street, lined with trees bedecked in twinkle lights.

Jacksonville Artwalk www.downtownjax.com

North Beach Art Walk http://www.nbaw.org/map-card

First Friday Art Walk http://artgalleriesofstaugustine.com

Artrageous Artwalk www.ameliaisland.com

[2]
Theater and Music

"A concert is like a feast day to me." –James Taylor

Florida Theater

A JACKSONVILLE LANDMARK since 1927, the Florida Theatre hosts over 200 cultural and entertainment events each year. It has been restored and listed on the National Register of Historic Places. When it first opened in the Roaring Twenties, it featured Vaudeville acts and silent movies. These days, you can see national recording artists, dance and live theater when the heavy velvet curtains open. Take time to read the signs in the lobby describing the building's rich history. If you'd rather not spring for a concert ticket, you can also enjoy the venue on Sunday afternoons during the Summer Movie Classic Series.

For a nearby restaurant with a date-friendly atmosphere, try Indochine. They serve Asian Fusion style offerings in a building with exposed brick walls, wood floors and large windows with city views. The noise level is low enough for a deep conversation with your significant other...or a shallow one, for that matter.

For a sexy place to have a drink after the show, walk across the street to Dos Gatos, recently highlighted by Void Magazine as one of "the top ten watering holes" in Jacksonville.

The Florida Theatre

128 E Forsyth St Jacksonville, FL 32205
(904) 355-5661 www.floridatheatre.com

Times-Union Center for the Performing Arts

The Times-Union Center for the Performing Arts is actually three performance facilities in one: the Robert E. Jacoby Symphony Hall, the Moran Theater and the C. Herman and Mary Virginia Terry Theater. A white, modern glass and block building perched on the banks of the Saint Johns River in downtown Jacksonville, the Times Union Center has been home to the Jacksonville Symphony Orchestra since 1997. In addition to the JSO, many other artists perform at the Times Union Center year round. Recent performances have featured Chris Botti, Darius Rucker, Vince Gill and Eddie Vedder. The Artist Series brings Broadway shows to the Moran Theater each year, and tickets can be purchased individually or in packages of multiple shows. Arrive early to enjoy a glass of wine in the two-story riverfront lobby and enjoy the night time city views.

For a nearby romantic dinner choice: try La Cena on North Laura Street. With a romantic atmosphere, a large selection of fine wine, and many tempting Italian delicacies on the menu, your evening will be complete. Due to their proximity to the Times Union Center, they are accustomed to serving theater patrons, and will be accommodating of your performance schedule.

Times-Union Center for the Performing Arts

300 Water St, Jacksonville, FL 32202 (904) 633-6110

Saint Augustine Amphitheatre

Originally built in 1965, the Saint Augustine Amphitheatre hosted Florida's official state play, "Cross and Sword" for 32 years. In 2002, the city undertook an extensive renovation of the property and turned it into a state-of-the-art performing arts venue, holding up to 4100 concert-goers. Nationally-known artists regularly play the venue. Recent concerts have included Chicago, The Smashing Pumpkins, Bob Dylan, LL Cool J and Peter Frampton. All concerts are held rain-or-shine, as most of the seats are covered, with the exception of the upper deck. Music concludes by 10 pm due to the proximity of neighborhoods. Although it is an amphitheatre, the venue has an intimate feel with seats located closer to the band than many other outdoor facilities. With impressive acoustics and sufficient video screens to give you an up-close look at performers, almost every seat is good. Bring cash for parking and beverages. Nearby restaurant recommendation: Gypsy Cab Co Restaurant

1340 A1A S St Augustine, FL 32080

(904) 471-1965 www.staugamphitheatre.com

[3]

Museums and History

> You know, I have a theory that hieroglyphics are just an ancient comic strip about a character named Sphinxy....
>
> ---When Harry Met Sally, (1989)

Museum of Science and History

THE MUSEUM OF SCIENCE AND HISTORY has a series called "MOSH After Dark" that is geared toward adults. These monthly events, which take place on Thursday nights, focus on different topics and usually feature a special speaker. Recent topics have included Jacksonville architecture, sustainable food, and, a personal favorite, beer brewing with Intuition Ale Works. Cost for these events varies from $5 to $15.

The museum also offers extended hours and reduced admission on Friday nights, as well as Cosmic Concerts, which they describe as "total-sensory entertainment where laser lights, high-def images and digital sound collide." Take advantage of the extended hours and browse the exhibits about local history. On date night, you can actually read all the signs instead of chasing after your children at breakneck speed. Suggested restaurant pairing: Bistro Aix

16 | Fifty First Coast Dates

233 S 1025 Museum Circle, Jacksonville Florida 32207

(904) 396-6674 www.themosh.org

The heart of Fernandina Beach on Amelia Island is Centre Street. Stroll down the sidewalk with your significant other and check out the many shops, galleries and restaurants. Just a couple blocks south on 3rd Street, you'll find the Amelia Island Museum of History. Located in the old Nassau County Jail, the museum houses relics of the "Isle of Eight Flags." Regular hours are from 10 to 4 , Monday through Saturday and 1- 4 on Sunday. However, special events in the evening include "Third on Third," a presentation of selected aspects of local history on the third Friday of every month at 6pm.For more thrills, try one of their Friday night ghost tours at 6pm. Led by a knowledgeable guide, you will hear chilling stories of local ghosts that might make you clutch your sweetie's hand for reassurance. Alternately, you could take one of their pub tours and end up clutching your date's hand for balance. Suggested romantic restaurant pairing: 29 South

233 S 3rd St, Fernandina Beach, FL 32034 (904) 261-7378

www.ameliamuseum.com

St Augustine Pirate and Treasure museum

Grab your wench (or pirate) and make a trip to the Pirate and Treasure Museum in St Augustine. Open until 8 pm daily, this collection of pirate artifacts includes one of the three surviving Jolly Roger flags left in the world and the world's only authentic pirate treasure chest. The museum is highly interactive and interesting for adults as well as younger visitors. The price of admission is a bit higher than some other local museums ($11-$15), but so is the quality of the experience. A lot of thought and research were put into this collection of impressive artifacts. Saint Johns County residents receive a significant discount with proof of residency.

Suggested romantic restaurant pairing: Tasting Room

12 S Castillo Drive, St Augustine Florida 32084 (877) 467-5863
www.thepiratemuseum.com

Ripley's Odditorium

Located in the historic Castle Warden building on San Marco Avenue, the Ripley's Odditorium houses many strange and unusual items from the collection of cartoonist and amateur anthropologist, Robert Ripley. Inside this medieval-looking building you will find a plethora of conversation-stimulating exhibits including the "Million Dollar Man," a statue made of shredded money, the giant erector-set Ferris wheel, a manatee made out of soda cans, and many more. Some descriptions overheard from visitors include: "cheesy and corny," and "freaky and weird." There is a room that appears to be moving, which might trick your vestibular system and send you to your knees. Beware the two-way mirror: on one side, there is a display challenging you to determine if you are among the percentage of the population that can roll their tongue. On the other side of the mirror is a crowd of people watching the goofy tourists make faces. The museum takes 1-2 hours to tour, and it is open everyday from 9 am to 8 pm. You can purchase combination tickets online which include a ride on the Ghost Train and a round of mini-golf for a full date night.

There are some good restaurants nearby, but after a visit to the Odditorium, perhaps you'll be in the mood for some unusual food that requires a dare to eat. Puffer fish, perhaps? Suggested restaurant pairing: The Olive Press

19 San Marco Avenue, Saint Augustine Florida 32084

(904) 824-1606   www.ripleys.com/staugustine

[4]

Gentleman's Choice

> Don't hate the player. Change the game.
>
> −*Think Like a Man* (2012)

Professional Sporting Events

Jacksonville has a number of options when it comes to professional sporting events. Beyond the obvious Jaguars games, you might be surprised by the other options you can find here.

The Jacksonville Jaguars have been much beloved (and often bemoaned) since the team was formed in 1995. Tickets to their games at EverBank field are around $60, and can be purchased online at www.jaguars.com. EverBank field has a variety of food options for purchase, although prices are predictably high. Recent changes allow ticket holders to bring their own food into the stadium. Take your date to a Jaguars game this season and "Stand United."

The Jacksonville Suns are a minor league baseball team, and they play right next door to EverBank Field at Bragan Field. The Suns are a AA feeder team for the Florida Marlins. It can be a lot of fun to spend an afternoon at the stadium with a beer and a hotdog, or you could attend one of their night games and try the Steak Me Out to the

Ballgame promotional, which includes a steak dinner. Tickets for Steak Me Out are $25. Regular price tickets start at $10.

The Jacksonville Sharks are an arena football team that plays at Sea Best Field. They are three time champions of the South Division of Arena Football League. Arena football is played indoors on a padded surface 85 feet by 50 yards long. These games are a lively experience, and tickets start at only $8. The season starts in March, so it's good for NFL fans in withdrawal. See www.sharkzone.com for the current season schedule and ticket information.

For something different, check out a rugby game. The Jacksonville Axemen play at the University of North Florida in a stadium full of 2500 screaming fans. Possibly due to the campus location, there is a party-like atmosphere at the games. Many promotions are offered, including full concessions, dollar beer, and prizes given away at halftime. The regular season takes place in May and June, and general admission tickets are only $5. See www.jaxaxe.com for more information.

If rugby isn't "different" enough for you, check out Jacksonville's lingerie football league. In what is billed as "the nation's fastest growing sports league," women play tackle football in Jacksonville Veterans Memorial Arena. Jacksonville recently acquired the team from Tampa and renamed them the Jacksonville Breeze. Advertisements for the team display woman wearing face paint and angry grimaces along with cleavage-baring corsets, but the new uniforms are a variation on standard football gear with shoulder pads and helmets...and a bare midriff. Tickets start at $10.

Jacksonville Jaguars at EverBank Field: (904) 633-6100
www.jaguars.com 1 EverBank Field Drive Jacksonville FL 32202

Jacksonville Suns Bragan Field/Baseball Grounds of Jacksonville: www.jaxsuns.com (904) 358-2846 301 A Phillip Randolph Blvd.

Jacksonville Sharks at Veterans Memorial Arena, 300 A Phillip Randolph Blvd (904) 630-3900 www.jaxsharks.com

Jacksonville Axemen at University of North Florida www.jaxaxe.com

Jackonville Breeze at Veterans Memorial Arena www.lflus.com/jacksonvillebreeze

Pool Hall

Looking for some action? Come pull out your stick and grab the rack. (Anonymous)

Some friendly competition over a pool table might liven up your next date. Q Ball Billiards is located in the Southside area of Jacksonville, in the strip mall with the giant T-Rex out front (another conversation starter). It is clean, smoke free, and has lots of tables. You'll probably see other couples there on dates as well. There's a full bar, food menu, and a reasonable hourly rate to play pool. Relatively decent players have reported that most of the tables are well leveled and have firm felt, whatever that means. You don't have to be a decent player to have fun here, however. Just remember to use the stick to hit the white ball, and knock the colored balls in the pockets (remembering if you are "solids" or "stripes"). Don't hit the white one in the pockets, or the black one (until the right moment—no one likes it when you sink your ball too soon).

First Coast Billiards is another pool hall located in Jacksonville Beach. They have 22 tables for you to choose from, so you don't have to be right on top of someone else (that comes after the date).

You might spot some really talented players at this location, so don't try to show off that behind-the-back move that never works. If you want to rough it a little more, you can play pool at Pete's Bar at the beach. There are only a few tables, but each game only costs a quarter. Pete's is a beach institution. It's been owned by the same family for 80 years. It's always smoky, and it's cash only. If you get tired of pool, you can switch to ping-pong. For reasons which should be obvious, do not reserve this date for a special occasion, like an anniversary. You will find yourself single again quite quickly. However, mutually consenting adults looking for a novel date night might find they have a good time shooting some pool.

Q Ball Billiards 10150 Beach Boulevard Jacksonville Florida www.qballjacksonville.com (904) 997-8222

First Coast Billiards 1226 Beach Boulevard Jacksonville Beach FL

Pete's Bar 117 First Street, Neptune Beach Florida 32266

(904) 249-9158

Gun Play

"The kick of running and jumping, dodging the paintball goes right back to your childhood." –William Shatner

Take out your aggression in an acceptable form when you try laser tag or paintball. Whether you're fed up with your mate or just had a rough week, a game of laser tag or paintball might be just what you need. At Adventure Landing in Jacksonville Beach, their laser tag room has an Area 51 theme. In the ready room, you'll be prepped for battle with a weapon and a vest that will keep track of how many shots you and your opponents have made. Little rooms and barrels offer places to lay in wait and ambush your beloved. Run around and feel like a kid again, or pretend you're Linda Hamilton in Terminator 2. At the end of the shooting match, you can see your score. Try not to brag too much if you left your date in the dust. For a larger scale experience, try paintball. In Jacksonville, Paintball Adventures offers paintball for individuals as well as groups. According to their website, Paintball Adventures is a fantastic woodsball/scenario facility....with 9 different courses including the 'Tiki' field, two forts (one with towers), bunkers, The Compound, two trail courses, and the very popular 'Blackhawk Down' field." Instruction and clean, well-maintained equipment is provided for a cost of about $50 for a full-day experience. Discounts are available for military personnel and their family, or check their facebook page for offers. Wearing camouflage is optional.

> Adventure Landing: 1944 Beach Landing, Jacksonville Beach, FL 32250 (904) 246-4386 www.adventurelanding.com
>
> Paintball Adventures 11850 Camden Road Jacksonville, Florida 32218 www.paintballadventures.com 904-645-7127

Baseball

> "Making love is just like hitting a baseball. You just gotta relax and concentrate." –Bull Durham (1988)

Having fun together is key to keeping romance alive. Skip the stuffy restaurant and non-interactive movie date, and go shag some balls. Visit your local batting cage. Seriously! It can be romantic as well as fun. Picture yourself, bat in hand, with your date snugly cozied up behind you, arms wrapped around you, helping you with your swing. Watch *Bull Durham* to get in the right mindset for this. First coast locations with batting cages include Mandarin Mill Family Golf & Batting Cages on Old San Jose Boulevard and Adventure Landing in Jacksonville Beach or Saint Augustine. You don't have to go to a batting cage to enjoy the great American pastime. You can get a couple of gloves and a ball, and have a game of catch in a nearby park. Pick one close to your house so that when you're done you can hit the showers as a team.

If you prefer to be a spectator, try a date at the Baseball Grounds of Jacksonville, home of the Jacksonville Suns. The regular season runs from April to September, and evening games are often held on Fridays and Saturdays. Popular promotions include the "Thursday Night Throwdown" with dollar drafts and "Steak Me Out to the Ballgame" when you can get a filet mignon, baked potato, salad, beverage and general admission ticket for $25. Some games will be followed by concerts featuring a variety of bands and performers. Check the schedule at www.jaxsuns.com.

Adventure Landing: 1944 Beach Boulevard, Jacksonville Beach, FL 32250 (904) 246-4386 www.adventurelanding.com

Baseball Grounds of Jacksonville www.milb.com (904) 358-2846 301 A Phillip Randolph Boulevard, Jacksonville Florida 32202

Mandarin Mill Family Golf and Games 10910 San Jose Boulevard Jacksonville Florida 32223 (904) 262-7888

[5]
Old School

Alyssa: *And this is where you take straight chicks on dates?*

Holden: *What, are you kidding? This place is like Spanish Fly!*

—Chasing Amy, (1997)

Arcade Night

Having fun together is a key element in keeping romance alive. Act like a kid again, and take your date to a local arcade such as Latitude 30 or Dave and Buster's.

Latitude 30 is an entertainment complex located in what was formerly a ToyRUs. It's huge, with multiple options for entertainment. Occupying most of the space is an upscale bowling alley, lined with white leather sofas and topped with big screen TVs. Wait staff will serve you drinks and even dinner in between spares and strikes. A smaller area in Latitude 30 houses a collection of arcade games, virtual racing, basketball hoops and skeeball. You and your date can grab side-by-side motorcycles and compete in a virtual race through Monte Carlo, or climb inside a video box and steer a virtual pirate ship. When you run out of tokens, check out the full-service cinegrill or catch a show at the comedy club. Suggested restaurant pairing: Bucca di Beppo

Dave and Buster's is always dark inside, so you can pretend you're in Vegas. It's loud and lined with many more video games than Latitude 30, but there are also pool tables and a restaurant inside if you get that unfortunate GAME OVER. On the other hand, maybe if he keeps playing, your date can win enough tickets to give you a giant stuffed Tweety Bird! Suggested restaurant pairing: Sushi Factory

Latitude 30: 10370 Phillips Highway, Jacksonville Florida 32256 (904) 365-5555 www.latthirty.com

Dave and Buster's 7025 Salisbury Road, Jacksonville FL 32256 (904)296-1525 www.daveandbusters.com

"Fore!" Play

For a Classic Date with a throw-back feel, try putt putt. You will have an opportunity to interact while you play, unlike your typical movie date, and enjoy some playful competition. In Jacksonville, Adventure Landing features a mini golf course dotted with plaster animals and water features that attract your ball with a magnetic quality. In Saint Augustine, with it's plethora of tourists, mini golf courses abound. Fiesta Falls has a tropical feel, with a large pirate ship planted in the middle. Across the bridge, you'll find Anastasia Mini Golf, open every day until 10 pm. Combination tickets with the Red Train ride are available at Bayfront Carpet Golf, which affords nice views of downtown. In Amelia Island, try your hand at Island Falls Adventure Golf. Watch out for the 7th hole, which you might over-muscle and send your ball flying into the road (unless you think this might impress your date, in which case, go for it).

Adventure Landing: 1944 Beach Boulevard, Jacksonville Beach, FL 32250 (904) 246-4386 www.adventurelanding.com

Fiesta Falls Miniature Golf: 818 A1A Beach Boulevard, St Augustine 32080 (904) 461-5571

Anastasia Mini Golf 701 Anastasia Boulevard, St Augustine 32080 (904) 825-0101

Dune Buggy Rides

If spa treatments and mud wraps aren't your idea of fun, perhaps, instead, you'd enjoy being covered in mud while riding a dune buggy. Dune Buggyz of Jacksonville is a dune buggy adventure park on the West Side. You and your date can rent one dune buggy or two, and get sprayed with mud as you swerve around the track. They recommend wearing old clothing and bringing a beach towel to protect your upholstery on the ride home. Eye protection is provided to keep the dust from flying in your eyes. Closed toe shoes are recommended, and women with long hair should tie it back. The cost is $25 for a 24 minute buggy ride. You must make reservations at least one hour before you plan to arrive, and a 50% deposit is required to hold your spot. This is a popular spot for birthday parties, so choose an off time for that or you might find yourself racing around the track with ten-year-olds. Baja Buggyz is open until 8pm on Friday and Saturday nights.

Baja Buggyz: 10622 103rd Street Jacksonville, Florida 32210

(904) 318-7398 www.bajabuggyz.com

Roller Skating

For a REALLY old-fashioned date, lace up your skates and hold hands for the couples only song. Year-round ice skating is available at Jacksonville Ice & Sportsplex. On Tuesdays from 7:30pm till 9:30pm, you can skate for $5 per person, including your skate rental.

Check their website for public skate times: www.jaxiceandsportsplex.com

If roller skating is more your speed, try Skate Station in Jacksonville. You'll be kickin it old skool style at this nostalgic skating rink. Nostalgic...run-down...it's all a matter of perspective. The lights are usually dim, so you might not notice the ravages of time here once the disco lights are flashing. Admission is $5 and includes skate rentals.

Jacksonville Ice & Sportsplex: 3605 Phillips Highway, Jacksonville (904) 399-3223 www.jaxiceandsportsplex.com

Skate Station Funworks: 3461 Kori Road Jacksonville Fl www.funworks.com (904) 880-7703

Bowling

Bowling alleys of today have radically changed from years gone by. Take for example, Luxury Bowling. "Luxury bowling?" you might say. "Isn't that an oxymoron?" At Latitude 30 in Jacksonville across from the Avenues Mall, it's a reality. White leather sofas flank each ball return. Gleaming bowling lanes are topped by a 120 foot digital video wall. Waiters and waitresses graciously serve you a full menu of food and beverages. But the shoes are still ugly.

For a special nighttime experience (isn't it always night time in a bowling alley?), try Cosmic Bowling. Beach Bowl, Bowl America and Jax Lanes feature Cosmic Bowling every Friday and Saturday night. During Cosmic Bowling, they dim the lights (vastly improving the atmosphere) and turn on the psychedelic black lights. A sound system plays music that will move you. Share a pitcher of beer with your date and let the romance begin.

Latitude 30: 10370 Phillips Highway, Jacksonville Florida 32256 (904) 365-5555 www.latthirty.com

*Beach Bowl: 818 Beach Boulevard, Jacksonville Beach FL 32250
www.beachbowljaxbeach.com (904) 249-9849*

Bowl America: 11141 Beach Boulevard Jacksonville Florida 32257 (904) 268-1511 www.bowl-america.com

Jax Lanes: 8720 Beach Boulevard, Jacksonville, Florida 32216 (904) 641-3133

[6]
Back to Nature

"Nature is about balance. All the world comes in pairs: yin and yang, right and wrong, men and women."

--Lara Croft, Tomb Raider (2003)

Picnic in the park

Did you know that Jacksonville has the largest system of public parks in the country? Parks occupy 111,669 acres in Jacksonville. Choose one of them and plan a romantic picnic for two. Check out www.coj.net for a searchable database of the 337 locations included in the JaxParks system. Losco Regional Park in Mandarin features huge live oaks, garlanded with Spanish moss, which could provide shade for your picnic blanket. In Riverside, Willowbranch Park is a verdant oasis in the middle of a trendy neighborhood. Located on Park Street, sandwiched in between Cherry Street and Willowbranch Avenue, shaded benches provide a comfortable spot to share a snack with your sweetie. As an added benefit, it's close enough to restaurants that you could get take out instead of packing a picnic basket.

In Saint Augustine, visit Canopy Shores Park, a 33 acre park located in the Shores Community along Christina Drive adjacent to the

Riverview Club. It's named for the large oak hammock canopy on the grounds. The park includes a 1.5 mile loop paved trail for walking, biking and birding.

City of Jacksonville Parks and Recreation www.coj.net

Willowbranch Rose Garden Park 2840 Park St Jacksonville 32205

Canopy Shores Park US 1 to Shores Boulevard to Christina Drive, St Augustine

St Johns County www.sjcfl.us

A Walk on the Beach

Sometimes it's relaxing to throw the organized events out the window and just take a walk on the beach. If you need something to do while you stroll, try looking for shells or shark's teeth. Sharks are constantly losing teeth and getting new ones, and with a careful eye you can spot these collector's items laying in the sand along the shoreline. Look for shiny black spots in the sand as you walk along. Shark's teeth are black, triangular, and appear shiny compared to the sand. It will take you a bit to train your eye to only see the black objects. Start a collection and after a few walks on the beach, you could be on your way to having a bowl of gleaming black shark teeth to accent your beachy decor. The beaches of Amelia Island are particularly known for having shark's teeth in the sand. You're chances of finding them are best at low tide.

Other beach walking activities include collecting seashells, bird watching, looking for dolphins or just holding hands.

Paddling (kayaks and Canoes, that is)

As aforementioned: we're surrounded by water here, people! There are some great places on the First Coast to launch your boat.

The Guana Tolomato Matanzas Estuarine Research Reserve, or GTMERR to her friends, is a beautiful region to explore by kayak or canoe. The GTMERR protects 73, 352 acres south of the City of Jacksonville in Saint Johns and Flagler Counties. At the north end, ten miles north of Saint Augustine on A1A in South Ponte Vedra, there are some good access points. Ripple Effect Ecotours operates guided tours which include the use of a single kayak, but tandem kayaks are available and much more romantic. Also, if you sit in the back of the tandem kayak, you can let your partner do most of the paddling and they won't notice as much. You might try a sunset paddle or a full moon trip. Their website says that they have glowing "firefly" kayaks. Current prices are $55 per person, which includes all necessary equipment and a two hour guided tour.

Travel farther south and you can "put-in" at Anastasia State Park. The same company, Ripple Effect Ecotours, also operates regularly scheduled kayak tours here in the serene waters of Salt Run. There is abundant marine life here, and you might spot a bottlenose dolphin or a manatee. Watch the sunset over the historic St. Augustine lighthouse when you try a sunset kayak tour. Another local company, Kayak St. Augustine offers a full moon St Augustine Lighthouse guided kayak tour every month. Make reservations first, and then meet at 5pm at the lighthouse for a "magical, mystical full moon experience on the salt run." Contact them at 904-315-8442.

Travel northward up our lovely coast and you will find Kayak Amelia. In addition to daytime kayak tours, sunset tours and full moon paddles, they offer something called "Firefly Tours." According to their website, "This is the closest we come to magic. For 4 weeks out of the year in the Spring, there is a special place where fireflies cover the forest floor in the park. On this tour we paddle as the sun sets and then our naturalists will lead you on a short, informative walk. As darkness falls the 'magic' begins." The fee is $60 per person." Bike ecotours, yoga classes (combined with kayaking to make them "yo-gak-ing" classes) and standing upright paddleboard (SUP) tours and instruction are among the many offerings here. Onsite, they have food, a gift shop and a restroom. Nearby is a paved bike trail you might want to check out; they also offer bike rentals.

Ripple Effect Ecotours www.rippleeffectecotours.com (904) 347-1565

Friends of the GTM Reserve 505 Guana River Road, Ponte Vedra Beach Florida 32082 (904) 823-4500 www.gtmnerr.org

Anastasia State Park www.floridastateparks.org/Anastasia 1340 Florida A1A, Saint Augustine, 32080 (904) 461-2033

Kayak St Augustine 904-315-8442 www.kayakingstaugustine.com St Augustine Lighthouse Park 442 Ocean Vista Ave St Augustine

Kayak Amelia www.kayakamelia.com 904-251-0016

13030 Heckscher Drive Jacksonville Florida 32226

[7]
Mood Music

"Music and love: they're going to bring you joy."

--The Last Song(2010)

Concerts al Fresco (and all free-o)

Take advantage of North Florida's mild weather by enjoying one of the many free outdoor concerts offered throughout the year. Since you don't have to pay for tickets, you should make this date really special by packing a fabulous picnic. Bring a bottle of wind, fancy appetizers and dessert to feed your sweetie. Plan a meal of finger food or bring disposable plates and silverware. At some of theses events, you will see people going all out: folding chairs and tables with tablecloths, candles, linen napkins and even flowers. Just remember, you have to be able to carry it all: Check the rules for allowed items first, as some will allow coolers and chairs, and some will not. Many will also offer food and drinks for purchase if you don't feel like packing.

As the weather warms up, you will be able to find more outdoor concerts around town. At the beaches, Seawalk Pavillion is the most common venue for events. Check www.jacksonvillebeach.org for a calendar of events. Every Mother's Day, the Navy Band performs a free concert of classical pops music. In summer, one Sunday night of every month, well-known jazz musicians perform as part of the Summer Jazz Concert Series.

In Downtown Jacksonville, free concerts are often held at Metropolitan Park, The Jacksonville Landing or Treaty Park. Every Spring, the Jacksonville Jazz Festival takes place in multiple locations downtown, and many are free. For an upscale (yet free!) event, don't miss the Jacksonville Symphony's Memorial Day weekend concert on the grounds of the Sawgrass Players Club in Ponte Vedra. You will definitely see a lot of very elaborate picnics at this annual event, so be sure to plan an equally impressive spread.

In Saint Augustine, free outdoor concerts are held at the Plaza de la Constitución. Beginning on Memorial Day and concluding on Labor Day, weekly performances of a variety of music styles take place every Thursday night at 7pm. The Memorial Day and Labor Day concerts start at 1pm. This event has been a local tradition for the past 22 years. Bring your chair and a picnic, but leave the wine at home: alcoholic beverages are prohibited at this event. On street parking is free after 5 pm (if you can find it) or you can park for $10 in the Historic Downtown Parking Facility.

Seawalk Pavillion, 1st St N and 1st Ave N, Jacksonville Beach FL
www.jacksonvillebeach.org

Metropolitan Park 1410 Gator Bowl Boulevard Jacksonville 32202

The Jacksonville Landing 1 Independent Drive Jacksonville 32202 www.jacksonvillelanding.com

Treaty Oak Park Prudential Drive Jacksonville 32202 www.coj.net

TPC Sawgrass, 110 Championship Way, Ponte Vedra Beach 32082 www.jaxsymphony.org

Plaza de la Constitucion St George Street St Augustine 32084 www.staugustinegovernment.com/sites/concerts-plaza

Jazz it up

The skyline of Saint Augustine is, for the most part, flat as the First Coast. Atop one of the few tall(ish) buildings you will find a local gem: "The Cellar Upstairs." This wine, jazz and blues bar tops off the San Sebastián Winery, located at 157 King Street. At this rooftop bar, you can order light appetizers, San Sebastián wine (of course) as well beer. Live music plays as you watch the sun set over the marsh. There is no cover charge. It opens at 4:30 pm on Fridays, and they are open for lunch on weekends. Check out their complimentary wine tastings and winery tours from 10-6 every day or 11-6 on Sunday. Local historians claim this area is the birthplace of American winemaking.

Each year in May, the city of Jacksonville shuts down some of their streets and sets the stage for the annual Jazz Festival. The festival lasts for four days, and most of the events are free. Stroll around with your sweetheart, enjoying local artists, vendors and food in the heart of Downtown Jacksonville. Hemming Plaza, The Jacksonville Landing and the Florida Theater all play host to some top Jazz performers. Tickets are required for some of the events. The weekend is capped off with a Sunday Jazz Brunch. See www.makeascenedowntown.com for a schedule of events or to purchase tickets.

The first Saturday night of each month, the Ritz hosts the Ritz Jazz Jamm featuring a different artist or group. Tickets are $25. The building also houses a museum focusing on the history and artistic talents of the African American community.

*San Sebastian Winery 157 King Street St Augustine FL 32084
www.sansebastianwinery.com (904) 826-1594*

Jacksonville Jazz Festival www.makeascenedowntown.com

*Ritz Theater Jazz Society 829 N Davis St Jacksonville 32202
www.ritzjacksonville.com (904) 632-5555*

Springing the Blues

Take advantage of the fabulous Spring weather here on the First Coast and schedule a date for "Springing the Blues" at the Seawalk Pavilion. It is the South's largest free blues festival on the ocean. The annual music festival always takes place on the first weekend in April, except when Easter falls on this weekend, in which case the festival will be held the following weekend.

Springing the Blues lasts for three days and features many renowned Blues musicians from around the country. You can bring a chair and stake out a spot on the lawn, but leave the cooler at home-- they're not allowed at this event. Instead, plan on taking advantage of the many food vendors on site. Mojo's Barbecue is one of the sponsors of the event, and what goes better with Blues than barbecue? Beer, of course. Alcoholic beverages are available for purchase as well. If you want to feel extra special, you may purchase premium seating. Different pricing is available for three-day or single-day passes, which are available at George's Music Store on Third Street. With your premium wristband, you will get seating near the stage with a beverage bar and *private* portable bathrooms (I guess the rest of us rabble will have to use the bathroom in public).

The attendance for this event has exceeded 250,000 for the last few years. Parking can be tricky. Paid parking lots will be monitored by the City of Jacksonville Beach for a fee of $10. Street parking can be found by the intrepid, or you could park off site and take the Beaches Trolley.

www.springingtheblues.com

Dance Club

The LOFT is likely the most hopping hotspot in Riverside these days. The open, funky decor and bumping bass keep the dance floor packed and the drinks flowing right up to closing time. In the main room you'll find an eclectic mix of people breaking it down to Katy Perry, MGMT, Juvenile and more underneath a sprawling spiderweb of rope and metal. Walk down a hallway at the rear of the space to find an intimate second bar with low lights and a different music selection; a little indie/80's hideaway from the bump and grind of the front room.

For those Vegas lovers out there, check out Club TSI and walk Jacksonville's semi-version of Fremont Street: the laser light tunnel in the alleyway. There's a screen with graphics and some laser lights that illuminate the tunnel. Zine-style artwork is plastered on the walls in a display of informality and funkiness. There's a small lounge area where you can chill and relax before you head inside to the actual club. Inside, there's a bar area to your right and the dance area to your left. The lighting system is touted as a "3-D lighting system." It looks like a pretty cool laser light show. There is an outdoor bar as well as the indoor bar. The pool table room is large and cozy, a great place to spend time chatting away from the stage, but still indoors. Restaurant suggestion: The Black Sheep

The Loft 925 King Street Jacksonville Fl 32204 www.loftjax.com
Club TSI 333 E Bay Street Jacksonville FL 32202
www.clubtsilive.blogspot.com

[8]
Nothin but Mammals

You made a woman meow?-When Harry Met Sally (1989)

Catty Shack Ranch Wildlife Sanctuary on the Northside of Jacksonville has evening hours for nighttime feeding events on selected Friday nights. You can view Siberian tigers, lions, cougars, spotted and black leopards, bobcats, coatimundis and arctic foxes. As night falls, it's feeding time! Over 450 pounds of meat gets distributed to resident predators, and plenty of roaring is sure to ensue. Hours are from 6 to 8pm, and feeding begins at 7:30. Maybe this display of ferocity will bring out the tiger in you when you get home.

Catty Shack Ranch 1860 Starrat Road Jacksonville FL 32226
www.cattyshack.org (904) 757-3603

Jacksonville Zoo and Gardens

The Jacksonville Zoo occupies 110 acres on the Trout River north of downtown Jacksonville. More than 2000 species of animals are represented and 1000 varieties of plants. Hours are from 9 to 5 every day except for Christmas, so this would be a daytime date unless you catch one of their special evening events. "After Dark Adventures" are offered periodically through the zoo's education department. A recent event for senior adults 55 and older included dinner, a zoo tour and information on special topics. Check the zoo's calendar for upcoming events. Walk hand in hand with your date along the tree-lined paths of the zoo. Share a snow cone to cool off on a hot day. Enjoy lunch at the Palm Plaza Café with a view of the Range of the Jaguars exhibit.

Jacksonville Zoo and Gardens

www.jacksonvillezoo.org

(904) 757-4463

370 Jacksonville Zoo Train, Jacksonville FL 32218

Horseback Ride on the Beach

Few things could be as romantic as a horseback ride on the beach. However, horses are only allowed on public beaches in certain locations in Florida (because few things can be as unromantic as taking a walk on the beach and stepping in horse doo-doo). Saint Johns County has restrictions on times of year and times of day that horseback riding is allowed on the beach.

Mickler's Landing is located in South Ponte Vedra on A1A and Mickler Road. The beach down here is mostly coquina, a crushed shell and sand mixture. Large, opulent homes line the coast, and dramatic waves cascade off shore where the coastline drops dramatically. Horseback riding is allowed here during specified hours. Sawgrass Stables is the primary provider of horseback riding on this beach. A guide leads riders on an hour-long ride, often scheduled to coincide with low tide. Sawgrass Stables charges $80 per person for an hour ride

On Amelia Island, Debbie Manser leads couples on horseback rides in beautiful Fernandina Beach. She meets riders at Peters Point Beach Front Park on S. Fletcher Avenue at low tide. She will personalize the ride based on your individual capabilities. Experienced riders may canter or trot along the water's edge. The cost is $80 per rider.

Some of the same companies that provide carriage tours in St. Augustine also provide horseback riding on the beach. Country Carriages will meet you at Surfside Park in Vilano Beach, just north of St Augustine. For $75 per person, a private guide will lead you on a one hour ride. You can make arrangements ahead of time if you'd like to stop for pictures or even to pop the question if you haven't done so already. Specify your comfort level with horses, and they will provide you with your perfect equine match. Rides consist of walking only; no cantering, galloping or trotting allowed.

Sawgrass Stables (904) 940-0020

Amelia Horseback Riding (904) 277-7047
www.ameliahorsebackriding.com

Country Carriages 36 Surfside Avenue St Augustine FL
www.countrycarriages.net (904) 826-1982

[9]

Eat, Drink and Be Merry

"You know the thing about good food--it brings people together." The Princess and the Frog, (2009)

Spice up your relationship with exotic food

Sometimes kicking the boring-date-habit can be as easy as trying a new exotic cuisine. A short list of some great international places to try in Jacksonville include: Buddha's Belly Thai, Pancitan ATBP Restaurant, Nile Ethiopian Restaurant, 13 Gypsies, Taverna Yamas and Bowl of Pho.

Unlike some international restaurants, the atmosphere at Buddha's Belly is cozy and romantic, which is one reason why I included it on this list. Nowadays, Thai food is not really that exotic. They accept reservations, which is good, because it's not romantic to wait an hour for a table. Showing you have the forethought to plan ahead will go a long way with the ladies. Share some Crab Rangoon or Chicken Satay as an appetizer. For your entrees, try the Pad Thai, Phra Ram or any one of the curries. The spicy cream shrimp are also huge, creamy and delicious. To go with the nicer atmosphere, you'll find higher prices here than you will at your neighborhood take-out joint, but it's worth it. The restaurant is conveniently located adjacent to the

Fred Astaire Dance Studio in case you really want to surprise your spouse by attending a dance class together.

Buddha's Belly Thai 301 10th Ave N Jacksonville Beach 32250
www.buddhathaibistro.com (904) 372-9149

Pancitan ATBP Restaurant has a casual atmosphere, not really date-like, but you can have fun trying unusual dishes here. The food is authentic Filipino cuisine. Start with the lumpia: the Filipino version of egg rolls fried to a delicious golden brown and served with a sweet and sour sauce. Next, go for the pancit: a noodle dish pan-fried with chicken, pork or fish. Menudo is a dish made for special occasions, cooked with chunks of potato, pork, chickpeas, onions and bell pepper. Pinakbet is a vegetable dish. Both are excellent here. After you've enjoyed home-cooking like a Filipino mama would make, you could walk down to the end of the shopping center and play pool at Q Ball. Incidentally, "ATBP" is a Filipino abbreviation roughly equivalent to "etc."

Pancitan ATBP Restaurant 10150 Beach Boulevard Jacksonville FL 32246 (904) 647-6746

At Tavernas Yamas, there's always a party going on. The question is, when with a date, do you *look* at the belly dancer as she undulates next to your table? Do you tip her? I solve that conundrum for my husband by tipping her myself. Then I give her a wink, just to make him think. The food here is Greek, and if you make it for happy hour, the appetizers are half price. Try the Saganaki, or flaming cheese. It sounds unusual, but it is very tasty on pita, and your waiter will light it on fire beside your table. All the Greek favorites are authentic and freshly made. For traditional Greek entrees, try the Pastitsio or the Moussaka. The lamb chops are marinated for 10 hours, seasoned with rosemary and perfectly cooked. The kabobs are juicy and well-seasoned, and the portions are enormous, so you might want to share. Don't forget to save room for dessert; the baklava will melt in your mouth.

Taverna Yamas 9753 Deer Lake Ct Jacksonville 32246
www.tavernayamas.com (904) 854-0426

Traditional Ethiopian cuisine is eaten with the hands. Share a handful of Alicha Wot ("alisha what??") with your true love and get out of your comfort zone. For your first time, try a meat sampler and a vegetable sampler. Tear off a piece of the pancake-like bread called injera, and use it to scoop up the meat and vegetables. Make sure you ask your server to give you a tour of the dishes: on my first visit, we asked our waitress to name each dish for us. When she said, "this is beef, this is pork, and this is tripe..." I made a mental note to stay away from 3 o'clock on that plate.

Nile Ethiopian Restaurant 6715 Powers Ave Ste 3 Jacksonville 32217

If you haven't heard the buzz about 13 Gypsies, you must be new in town. This little diner in Riverside has rave reviews. They serve Spanish cuisine from the Basque region. They only have a few tables, so call ahead to make reservations. Most of the items on the menu are tapas, so order a few different things to share, and you can try them all. They make their own bread and cheese here, so you should choose a starter that includes those two elements. The Roman style gnocchi is not-to-be-missed, so I'd go with that next. Don't expect the gnocchi to look like little pasta pockets. Roman style means that they are baked in strips, which, according to the menu is the original, authentic way to make it. Mushrooms Sevilla are delicious and buttery. The empanada of the day is always good, and might serve to fill in the gaps left by nibbling on tapas. Save room for the tres leches dessert, though. After dinner, you might want to walk down the block and enjoy a cup of coffee at the nearby Bold Bean Coffee Roasters. They roast their own coffee, and sometimes host live music.

> *13 Gypsies 887 Stockton Street Jacksonville 32204 (904) 389-0330 www.13gypsies.com*

Bowl of Pho is located in a funky strip mall on Old Baymeadows Road, but don't let that sway you. Inside, the dining room is very Zen. Bamboo, fish tanks and a soothing color scheme combine to make a calming atmosphere. Start out with the shrimp spring rolls and some boba tea. Try one of the many combinations of pho (P11 is good). Don't be afraid to spruce it up with the options before you: fresh Thai basil, lime slices and bean sprouts are provided when your soup is served. Spicy sauces are always placed on the tables, and really give it that extra kick. After dinner, walk around the corner to The Coffee Grinder: a locally-owned coffee lounge that actually stays open late. They serve alcohol as well as coffee, and they often have musical entertainment ...sometimes *loud* musical entertainment.

> *Bowl of Pho 9902 Old Baymeadows Rd Jacksonville Florida 32256 (904) 646-4455*

Northward on the First Coast, Amelia Island is the "Isle of Eight Flags," so they one could expect to find some different culinary experiences here as well. In the historic part of town, Espana serves Basque Spanish cuisine and tapas. Try the mussels with chorizo or the Portuguese fisherman's stew. Down the street, Bonito Grill and Sushi has a very zen-like atmosphere and serves Asian Fusion cuisine. A few blocks south, on Elm Street, MERGE serves eclectic fare in a cool atmosphere. Try the wild boar for bragging rights, but save room for crème brulee cheesecake. Be sure to make a reservation, as this place is popular with locals and visitors.

Espana 22 S 4th St Fernandina, FL 32034 (904) 261-7700 www.espanadowntown.com

Bonito Grill and Sushi 614 Centre St Fernandina, FL 32034 www.bonitogrillandsushi.com (904) 261-0508

MERGE 510 S 8th Street Fernandina, FL 32034 (904) 277-8797

Saint Augustine is a popular honeymoon spot, and all that hand-holding just might inspire you. For exotic fare, you could try French food at Le Pavilion in Uptown. Practice your best French accent as you order for your date. Double-dog-dare him to eat an escargot. After dessert, you might like to walk around this part of town and explore a few antique shops. If Spanish food is more your taste, you are in the right place. Saint Augustine was founded by the Spanish, after all. Try Columbia Restaurant on George Street. Order your paella right away, as it takes 30 minutes to prepare. Ensconced in a courtyard with a bubbling fountain, you might forget that you are surrounded by tourists.

Despite it's location in the midst of a Spanish colony, Japanese restaurant "Spy" in St Augustine reportedly serves the best sushi in all of North Florida. You might also sample the duck egg rolls or coconut lemongrass sake. After dinner, walk up Hypolita Street and have a gourmet popsicle for dessert, then take a romantic walk along the water.

Le Pavilion 45 San Marco Ave St Augustine 32095 (904) 824-6202 www.lepav.com

Columbia Restaurant 98 St George Street St Augustine 32084 www.columbiarestaurant.com (904) 824-3341

Spy 21 Hyplolita Street St Augustine 32084 (904) 819-5637
www.spyglobalcuisine.com

The Hyppo 48 Charlotte Street St Augustine 32084 (904) 217-7853

Waterfront Dining

There are so many options for waterfront dining on the First Coast. Nothing compares to the romance of a dinner on the oceanfront or by the river. Make your reservations in advance and be sure to make a special request for a table with a view: there's nothing worse than choosing a lovely waterfront restaurant and getting seated in an interior booth by the kitchen. Give some thought to the time of year and time of day: there's not much point in an ocean view table when it is pitch black outside. After dinner, take a romantic stroll by the water.

Cap's on the Water is located off the Coastal Highway between South Ponte Vedra and Vilano Beach. It has a lovely waterfront location on the Tolomato River. Large trees shade the outdoor seating area and come alive with tiny white lights at night. Overlooking the water to the west provides a beautiful sunset view. There can be a lengthy wait for tables on weekend evenings, so plan to take it slow. Order a glass of wine while you wait, and enjoy the scenery. For dinner, try the vanilla grouper, or any of the other tempting seafood dishes.

Cap's on the Water 4325 Myrtle Street St Augustine 32084
www.capsonthewater.com (904) 824-8794

The Reef is also located on the Coastal Highway south of Ponte Vedra, however, it is oceanfront. Inside, you'll see floor-to-ceiling windows allowing a beautiful view of the Atlantic. Try the crab cakes and the fried green tomatoes. If you arrive during happy hour, appetizers are half price, and you'll have plenty of daylight to enjoy the view. After dinner, take a romantic walk along the ocean and hold hands.

The Reef 4100 Coastal Highway St Augustine 32095
www.thereefstaugustine.com (904) 824-8008

Brett's Waterway Cafe in Fernandina overlooks the scenic Amelia River. While you wait for your table to be ready, rock in the rocking chairs on the porch overlooking the water, and picture yourself and your spouse at 80 years old, still rocking side-by-side. Sample the shrimp and grits while you watch the shrimp boats outside your window--possibly the same boats that caught your dinner! Finish your meal with key lime pie: a touch of tartness, but mostly sweet, just like marriage.

Brett's Waterway Café 1 South Front St Fernandina, FL 32034
(904) 261-2660

Downtown in Jacksonville, a couple of restaurants offer a scenic view of the river and the nighttime skyline. Try the River City Brewing Company or the Chart House, both located on the South bank. If you go to the Chart House, make sure to let your server know you'll have the molten lava cake for dessert when you order your entree--it takes extra time to prepare, but it's worth it!

River City Brewing Company 835 Museum Cir Jacksonville 32207 www.rivercitybrew.com (904) 398-2299

Chart House 1501 Riverplace Boulevard Jacksonville 32207
(904) 398-3353 www.chart-house.com

Many people are unaware that 619 Ocean View, the oceanfront restaurant at the Cabana Club in Ponte Vedra is open to the public. This restaurant is beautiful, inside and out. With a magnificent ocean view, you will definitely want a window seat. When the sun is shining, enjoy the wonderful wrap-around deck outside. The food is well-prepared and delicious, but pricey--this is a special occasion spot for most. Try the scallops for dinner--they get rave reviews. The caramel gelato with pretzel crust is a surprising taste combination that you might enjoy for dessert. Slip down to the ocean before you retrieve your car from the valet, and don't leave without sand in your shoes (or, if you're feeling daring, in other unmentionable areas).

619 Ocean View 619 Ponte Vedra Blvd, Ponte Vedra Beach 32082 (904) 285-6198 www.sawgrassmarriott.com/dining/619-oceanview

Fondue for Two

What kind of restaurant makes you cook your own food?

–Lost in Translation (2003)

At traditional restaurants you just order separate entrees, eat, and then leave. At The Melting Pot, you select a three or four-course meal for two. Start out simply, with a cheese fondue. Try the traditional Swiss cheese fondue which has a splash of Kirshwasser, a cherry brandy that balances the sharpness of the cheese. For your main course, choose the meats and the style of cooking you'd prefer, including vegetable broth, mojo bouillon, coq au vin or the traditional oil-based Bourguignon style. You cook the meats you selected (steak, shrimp or chicken)in a fondue pot on the table top burner built into your table. A variety of sauces are offered, and you can compare your favorite combinations. You definitely want to save room for dessert, however. Choose the type of chocolate you prefer from a selection of dark, white or milk chocolate in varying combinations. When it has melted into creamy goodness, you can feed your sweetheart strawberries, cheesecake and brownies dipped in chocolate.

This is a special occasion favorite, with prices to match, so keep an eye out for the special offers sometimes mailed out close to holidays. Be sure to make reservations, as the wait can be quite long if you haven't planned ahead. You might want to request a table on "Lover's Lane:" a hallway lined with intimate tables for two.

The Melting Pot 7860 Gate Parkway Jacksonville 32256
www.meltingpot.com (904)642-4900

Taste the First Coast

Why settle for one restaurant? Check out one of the First Coast's culinary tasting events, and sample fare from a multitude of the best restaurants in town.

On Amelia Island, the Taste of Amelia takes place annually in the fall at the Amelia Island Plantation. A tradition spanning over twenty years, this culinary fair showcases the skills of the best local chefs. Featuring dozens of restaurants each year, this event features wine tastings and silent auctions as well as food. Money raised by ticket sales and auctions will benefit the Nassau County Volunteer Center. This is somewhat of a gala event, usually held at the Omni, which often offers discounted rates for the event if you decide to make it a an overnight event.

The annual Taste of Saint Augustine is a bit more laid-back. Held at the Saint Augustine Amphitheater in April, this event features live bands and a ticket cost of only 5 dollars. In addition to the entry price, food tickets cost $1. Trade tickets for samples of signature dishes from over 30 local restaurants. They will compete to win the coveted "Best of Taste of Saint Augustine" award. All proceeds benefit local nonprofit, Epic Behavioral Healthcare.

Tickets for Taste of Amelia: www.volunteernassau.org

Tickets for Taste of St Augustine:
www.epicbh.org/tasteofstaugustine.html

Wine Tasting

Haven't you always wanted to know the proper way to drink wine? When offered the first taste of a bottle at a restaurant, are you unsure what to do? Sniff the cork? Swish and spit? A wine tasting might be your first step in developing your knowledge of the grape. In addition, many of the wine tastings around town take place in the evenings on Friday or Saturday nights, and many are complimentary. The perfect cheap date!

In Amelia Island, "A Taste of Wine by Steve" is located at 5174 First Coast Highway. They offer complimentary tastings every Friday from 5 to 7 pm, as well as other special events throughout the year. You will get the opportunity to sample wines and food that you may have never tasted before: A Taste of Wine by Steve specializes in hard-to-find wines. They also do wine dinners and ticketed events at local spots like Fernandina Beach Golf Club. They can even organize private events in your home. Check the website for more details: www.atasteofwinebysteve.com

PRP Wine International offers wine tastings around Jacksonville. They have been featured at the Up and Cummer's Art After Hours quarterly events. The Up and Cummers are a group of young professionals who meet for evening events at the Cummer. If you are not a member, you may still purchase tickets for $10 by calling (904) 889-6004 or going online at www.cummer.org/programs-events.

Riverside Village Wine Shop offers free wine tastings every Friday night. Located at 1035 Park Street, this business looks like an ordinary liquor store from outside, but there is a bar in the back. Inside it can be quite crowded as this place is quite popular with the locals. The staff is very knowledgeable about wine without the attitude. Occasionally, wine distributors are on site to answer your questions and introduce you to new wines. After you sample a few, you won't have far to walk to Riverside's restaurants. Try Mossfire Grill or Black Sheep Restaurant.

In Saint Augustine, San Sebastian winery offers complimentary wine tastings and tours of their winery seven days a week. It is located in one of Henry Flagler's old East Coast Railway buildings, at 157 King Street. Check their website to confirm tour hours (10-6 Monday through Saturday and 11 to 6 on Sunday...so you can go to church first, I guess).

A Taste of Wine by Steve 5174 First Coast Hwy Fernandina 32034 www.atasteofwinebysteve.com (866) 709-9665

PRP Wine International www.prpwine.com (904) 646-4106

Cummer's Art After Hours www.cummer.org/programs-events

Riverside Village Wine Shop 1035 Park Street Riverside 32204 www.riversideliquors.biz (904) 356-4517

San Sebastian Winery 157 King Street St Augustine, Florida www.sansebastianwinery.com (904) 826-1594

Comedy Club

For some cheap laughs and expensive drinks, try one of Jacksonville's comedy clubs on your next date night. Oddly located in the Ramada hotel in Mandarin, the Comedy Zone features celebrity performers, up-and-comers and local comedic talent in a kitschy environment. Walk into the lobby and you'll find yourself surrounded by photos of mostly-forgotten stand up comedians from the past. The auditorium is small, filled with clusters of tables and chairs, and lined with more odd paintings of comedians. Tickets are cheap, or even free, but there is usually a minimum drink order required. The food is over-priced as well, so treat your date to a romantic dinner elsewhere.

Try Enza's Italian Restaurant, just up the road on San Jose Boulevard.

For a slightly swankier environment, try Latitude Live at Latitude 30, featuring national talent in a "Vegas-style" 170 seat auditorium. Tickets are $10, and a full menu is available with full dining service. Shows are every Friday and Saturday night at 7:30. Doors open at 6:30.

Comedy Club of Jacksonville on Beach Boulevard boasts that they have top-quality food made with only fresh ingredients and priced at 10 dollars or less. They bring comedy to the menu with their Food on a Shtick: chicken, steak and shrimp kabobs. Tempting desserts from Cinotti's will make you smile, even if the comedian doesn't. They offer spacious seating in a non-smoking environment, and they are the only local comedy club to provide ratings (PG-13 Language, R-rated content) in case your idea of a fun evening doesn't involve listening to someone drop the f-bomb.

The Comedy Zone 3130 Hartley Rd Jacksonville FL 32257
www.comedyzone.com (904) 292-4242

Latitude 30 10370 Phillips Highway, Jacksonville Florida 32256
(904) 365-5555 www.latthirty.com

Comedy Club of Jacksonville 11000 Beach Blvd Jacksonville 32246 www.jacksonvillecomedy.com (904) 646-HAPPY

Scarlett and Rhett's

Situated snugly side-by-side on the corner of Hypolita and Cordova in historic Saint Augustine you will find Scarlett O'Hara's and Rhett's Piano Bar. While common logic generally advises "ladies first," in this case, start with Rhett's. An elegantly-decorated brasserie with two floors and a roaring 20's atmosphere, Rhett's features fine dining accompanied by talented pianists. Savor the opportunity to listen to amazing live music and enjoy each other's company. The atmosphere is romantic--even more so when you request "your" song to the piano player. For starters, try the goat cheese crouton, a recipe straight from New Orleans.

After dinner, head next door for drinks in a completely different atmosphere. You know that Scarlett was never much of a lady. The restaurant/bar that bears her name can sometimes take on a raucous atmosphere. Try the Scarlett Red beer if you want to stick with the theme, or if you don't feel like imbibing, the key lime pie is a treat. Sit on the porch and enjoy the evening, or explore the dim, cavernous interior of this 19th century home. Legend has it that the former owner died upstairs in his bathtub, and his spirit sometimes makes itself known. Live music is offered most nights, and there is a small cover charge.

Scarlett O'Hara's 70 Hypolita Street St Augustine 32084
www.scarlettoharas.net (904) 824-6535

Rhett's 66 Hypolita Street St Augustine 32084 (904) 825-0502
www.rhetts.com

Cuban Food and Dancing

A little piece of Havana in Jacksonville, Havana Jax Cuban restaurant and Cuba Libre, the adjacent nightclub offer complimentary Latin dance lessons every Friday night. Start the evening at Havana Jax Cafe with some Cuban food. This family-run establishment has been part of Jacksonville since 1994. They serve large portions of delicious, authentic recipes from Old Havana. Try the green plantains and pork chicharones, the Bolce Asado or the famous paella. Finish your meal with some bold Cuban coffee and flan and let your food settle, then step over to Cuba Libre to kick up your heels. A $10 cover charge includes a group dance lesson from 9:00 to 10:00pm.

On their website, owner Silvia Pulido explains that she was inspired to open a nightclub next to the restaurant when her children returned from a work trip to Costa Rica, where they enjoyed the Latin nightlife. She describes it as "a high-end nightclub infused with the culture and the rhythm of her native Latin culture. Cuba Libre offers Latin music; a dance floor; a large-screen projection television; plush leather couches; beautiful, native artwork; and exotic drinks native to the Caribbean."

After an evening at Cuba Libre (and a few of their namesake drinks), and your partner will be ready for some smooth moves. Cuba Libre: 2578 Atlantic Boulevard Jacksonville 32207 (904) 399-0609 www.cubalibrebar.com

[10]

Dinner and a Movie

A good film is when the price of the dinner, the theatre and the babysitter were worth it.

--Alfred Hitchcock

Cinema Grill

If the idea of choosing a restaurant AND a movie (sigh) is too much for you, or if you just like to drink beer while you watch the latest blockbuster, then check out one of the First Coast's cinema/grills.

In San Marco, the historic San Marco Theater offers current movies and a full menu of pizza, subs, quesadillas and such, as well as beer and wine. You should arrive early to place your order before the movie starts. You will be given a buzzer that will let you know when your food is ready. You return to the window to pick up your order. Some seats have small tables conveniently located. They don't show a lot of previews, so the movie actually starts when the published schedule at www.sanmarcotheatre.com says it will.

In nearby 5 points, the Sun Ray Cinema shows the latest movies as well as some artsy ones. Their menu includes pizza, Cuban sandwiches and hotdogs. They also give you a pager to let you know when your food is ready, but they will bring your order to you, guided by the gentle glow of your pager. They have local beers on tap, a selection of wine, and you can even get a bottle of bubbly (or a bucket of PBR, depending on how you roll). Tickets can be purchased at www.sunraycinema.com.

In Saint Augustine, the Pot Belly Cinema offers the cinema/grill experience in a quirky, historical setting. Not a modern theater by any stretch of the imagination, this multi-screen cinema shows many indie films in a quaint setting. Beer and snacks are available for purchase, and table service is offered for some showings.

San Marco Theatre 1996 San Marco Blvd Jacksonville Fl 32207 (904) 396-4845 www.sanmarcotheatre.com

SunRay Cinema 1028 Park Street Jacksonville 32204 www.sunraycinema.com (904) 359-0047

Pot Belly Cinema 36 Granada Street St Augustine 32084 (904) 829-3101

Moonlight Movies

Thanks to our beautiful Florida weather, we have many options for outdoor movies. Take advantage of one of them this season.

The City of Jacksonville Beach holds their annual Moonlight Movies series at Seawalk Pavilion, starting at the end of May every year. Bring your lawn chairs or spread out a blanket and enjoy a movie under the stars with the sound of the waves nearby. Pack a picnic and make an evening out of it (with the added benefit of staking out your spot early). Films begin at 9pm.

The City of Jacksonville hosts an outdoor movie series every Spring called Movies in the Park. The annual event is held on the South bank of the Saint Johns River adjacent to the Wyndham Jacksonville Riverwalk Hotel. Plenty of free parking is available at the Wyndham parking lot, accessible from Prudential Drive. This movie series features family-friendly movies, so there will probably be plenty of children there. Stake out your spot early and bring dinner with you. Plenty of local restaurants offer tasty take out options.

At the Saint Augustine Amphitheater, the Night Owl Cinema Series features free movies every year. Parking is free, and seating is provided for this one, so you won't need lawn chairs. No outside food is permitted. Gates open at 6:30, and the movie starts at 8:00. The concession stand serves pizza, burgers, hot dogs and nachos along with those movie favorites, popcorn and candy.

Moonlight Movies www.jacksonvillebeach.org

Movies in the Park www.downtownjacksonville.com

Saint Augustine Amphitheatre www.staugamphitheatre.com
(904) 471-1965 1340 A1A S. Saint Augustine FL 32080

[11]

Learning Together

Your aim is almost as bad as your cooking, Sweetheart.

--Mr. and Mrs. Smith (2005)

Cooking for Two

Instead of having another dinner-and-a-movie date, why not learn how to cook for yourself? Attend a local cooking class specially designed for couples, and see if you can heat things up on your next date.

Publix at San Jose Boulevard offers a cooking school with a variety of classes. A couple's class featuring different cuisines and cooking styles takes place two evenings every month. Recent offerings have included "Thai for Two," "Spring Grilling" and "Seafood Grill Out." You'll get the opportunity to learn a new cooking technique while enjoying a lot more interaction than you'd get in a movie theater. Picture yourself offering your sweetie a sample from your cooking spoon. This is the date that keeps on giving: you can try your new recipe at home the next time you're staying in. Additional classes to try include the wine pairings classes or the celebrity chef series.

Williams Sonoma also offers cooking classes at all of their store locations. Jacksonville has two locations: one at the Avenues Mall (904-538-0750) and one at the Town Center (904-998-4304). Classes include demonstrations and samples of featured dishes, as well as printed recipes to take home with you. Pan Roasting, Seasonal Desserts and Holiday Brunch Menus are among the recent offerings. Call to get an updated schedule and make reservations.

Blue Bamboo offers a fun, interactive cooking class each month on Saturdays from 10 to noon. Chef Dennis Chan, author of *Hip Asian Comfort Food*, is an entertaining instructor as well as an award-winning chef. Each month features a different theme, and recent offerings have included Dim Sum Twists, Spring Market Cooking and Exotic Asian Veggies.

Sustainable Springfield offers a seasonal cooking class focused on using farm-fresh, in-season ingredients. Executive chefs from Black Sheep, MAZA, The Floridian and BB's will teach a class at the beginning of each season about what is coming in season and how to cook with it. You could follow up this date with a trip to the farmers market to pick up some fresh, local produce. This non-profit fundraiser benefits Sustainable Springfield, an organization that strives to turn local liabilities into local assets such as community gardens and orchards.

Williams Sonoma Avenues Mall (904)538-0750, Town Center (904)998-4304

Blue Bamboo 3820 Southside Blvd Jacksonville 32216 (904) 646-1478 www.bluebamboojacksonville.com

Sustainable Springfield www.sustainablespringfield.com

Publix Apron's Cooking School (904) 288-6660 www.publix.com 10500 San Jose Blvd #36 Jacksonville 32257

Martial Arts

When you feel like punching your partner, schedule a martial arts date instead. It might sound strange, but when you think about it, there can be a lot of friendly physical contact involved. For instance, when you learn holds, you have your arms wrapped around your opponent, I mean partner. Gary Chapman, author of *The Five Love Languages* says that physical touch can make or break a relationship. Looking for unique and new ways to share physical touch? Try a choke hold.

If you'd like to have some fun with pugilistic arts without choke holds, try a boxing class. TITLE Boxing Club on San Pablo and Beach Boulevard offers a first lesson for free. You and your date can work the punching bag and get a great workout. Family memberships allow both of you to come in and workout in unlimited classes. Competitive boxers lead the classes, and help you put those big gloves on too.

There are many styles of martial arts: karate, judo, jiu jitsu, Krav Maga, aikido, and Taekwondo to name a few. Practicing any of these together can put a renewed energy back into your relationship. Many local martial arts studios offer free or reduced rate introductory classes, so you can try this date idea without any commitment.

Authors Note: Couples with serious relationship or aggression issues should not try this date. This suggestion was meant for fun and novelty.

TITLE Boxing Club 14286 Beach Blvd Jacksonville, FL 32250

(904) 256-9607 www.titleboxingclub.com

Parallel Painting

Think you can't create something together as a couple? *Yes You Canvas! Yes You Canvas* is located at the intersection of San Jose and University Boulevard. An artist teaches a classroom of amateur Picassos how to paint a canvas to look like his sample. Choose the painting you want to make ahead of time on their website, and make a reservation. Since you will both be painting the same thing, consider an image that can be slightly altered to look good displayed as a pair: for example, two flowers in complementary colors or mirror-image palm trees. See www.yesyoucanvas.com to choose your new sofa-topping display. You can bring a bottle of wine to sip while you paint.

Instead of painting a canvas, try painting pottery. *Doing Dishes Pottery Studios* on San Jose Boulevard has evening hours and a large selection of ceramic items to choose from. Paint a matching set of mugs for your morning coffee, or create individual items. It doesn't matter what you paint, as long as you are sitting together and interacting while you paint. Just don't criticize your partner's painting skills. Practice saying, "That looks so good, Honey!" You really might need this phrase if you sip too much wine while working and your painting precision suffers. (Wine and snacks are also allowed here.) If you think you're not creative enough, they have idea books and helpful artists on hand to assist.

At Arts Ignited, you can not only try your hand at painting pottery, you can play in clay. Arts Ignited offers paint-your-own-pottery with no studio fees, classes in fused glass for beginners and clay available on Monday and Wednesday nights to build your own pottery. All the clay tools, forms and other tools needed are provided.

Yes You Canvas! 2777-32 University Blvd W. Jacksonville 32217 (904) 993-9047 www.yesyoucan.com

Doing Dishes 5619 San Jose Blvd Jacksonville 32207 (904) 730-3729 Avondale 3568 St Johns Ave Jacksonville 32205 (904) 388-7088 www.doingdishes.com

Arts Ignited Center www.artsignited.com (904) 638-6692 Oakleaf 9715 Crosshill Boulevard Jacksonville 32222

Board? (surfboard, that is) Take a lesson!

To keep your relationship afloat, you need to stay on your feet. Take a lesson together and learn surfing or Stand Up Paddleboard (that's "SUP," dude), and learn a new skill while having fun in the sun. In addition, if it turns out that you both enjoy the sport, you will have something new to do together in the future. North Florida offers many beautiful spots to get on the water.

Jax Surf Training offers private and group surfing, SUP, and fitness classes at the beach or on the Intracoastal Waterway. They offer a money back guarantee that their certified instructors will have you up and paddling in one lesson. The beginner lesson teaches basic skills like board handling, water entry, standing up, paddling and turning. They start out on placid waters off the Intracoastal. They recommend starting out with a bigger board, and they will provide one that is suitable for your lesson, as well as other equipment such as a paddle, leash, flotation device and even a wetsuit if needed. A 90 minute SUP lesson will cost you $75 each, or you can purchase gift certificates or packages of 5-10 lessons.

If you've always dreamed of hanging ten, Jax Surf Training also offers private surf lessons at the beach for the same rate. They claim: "In one lesson, we can have you standing or see what we need to do to get you there." It is likely that it will take more than one lesson to become a big kahuna, so this might end up being a series of dates after you get a taste of it.

In Amelia Island, Kayak Amelia offers Stand Up Paddleboard instruction during their SUP eco tours. They have beginner-friendly boards, and only utilize flat water sandy locations. The tours last for 2 hours. Orientation, instruction and a tour of the scenic area between Amelia Island and Talbot Island are included. You will pause for breaks on sandbars and beaches, and they'll even give you a cookie. Cost for the tour is $55 per person.

To learn how to surf a wave in Saint Augustine, contact the people at St Augustine Surf. They teach surfing to all ages, and a 90 minute surf lesson for 1-4 people will cost $60 per student. They provide a

CPR certified instructor and use of a surfboard, and say that you will certainly be able to stand up and ride a wave before the day is done.

For SUP in the St Augustine area, try "Let's Go Standup." In addition to private lessons, they schedule meetups and tours in different locations including Salt Run, Washington State Park, Moses Creek and others. Find their schedule online. They offer first-timer-friendly tours on Saturday mornings, or try a full moon paddles leaving from the Saint Augustine lighthouse. You'll need to bring a headlamp, glow stick or some other light source. Bring your own board, or rent one for $30. Don't forget the bug spray!

Jax Surf Training www.jacksonvillesurftraining.com

(904) 435-7873

Kayak Amelia www.kayakamelia.com (904)251-0016

St Augustine Surf www.staugustinesurf.com (904) 294-SURF

"Let's Go Standup" www.meetup.com/paddleboard-saint-augustine

Dance Lesson

Perhaps, like me, you have forced your mate to watch *Dancing with the Stars* (competition, results show, competition recap show...), and now you are inspired to learn how to dance as well as a running back on reality TV. Work on your smooth moves together by taking a dance class. Dancing together can improve your health, communication and confidence, while also providing an opportunity for relaxation and fun. Sequins are not required.

Kaluby's Dance Club offers private dance lessons for couples. Lessons are 45 minutes long, and take place in the main ballroom, where you will have your own instructor. Other individuals or couples may be receiving instruction at the same time from other instructors in the same room; "private" means you have your own teacher, not that you are alone in the room. However, they will all be looking at their feet, so no worries. Kaluby says: "Dancing is a physical activity as well as a great contact sport. Every minute you can spend moving your body to music, whether alone or with a partner, will work wonders for your progress." Your first lesson is free when you register online or by phone.

If you are more of a traditionalist, learn dancing the Fred Astaire way. At Fred Astaire Dance Studios, they offer private lessons, group lessons and practice lessons. In your first lesson, you will learn the basic elements of which all dances are made, and start working your way up into many types of ballroom dancing, including the waltz, fox-trot, cha-cha, merengue and more! Fred Astaire Dance Studios in Jacksonville offer an introductory special.

Kaluby's 8221 Southside Blvd Jacksonville 32256 (904)338-9200 and 13245-7 Atlantic Boulevard Jacksonville 32225 (904)221-1331 www.kalubys.com

Fred Astaire Dance Studios www.fredastairejacksonville.com

315 10th Ave N Jacksonville Beach 32250

8732 Lone Star Rd Jacksonville 32211

[12]

Tour the Town

The real voyage of discovery consists not in seeking new landscapes but in having new eyes. —Marcel Proust

River Cruises

The First Coast is surrounded by water, so enjoy our beautiful region on a river cruise. Amelia River Cruises offers romantic sunset cruises that leave from the Fernandina Harbor Marina. Sunset cruises are "no-kids-allowed," and it's BYOB! Bring a picnic basket with snacks, cups, a bottle of wine (don't forget the corkscrew!) and your camera. Musicians come along for the ride and play laid-back tunes while the marshlands roll by. The boat is filled with rows of front-facing seats, but after a while people begin to stand up, walk around and mingle. It's like a floating cocktail party. Cruise across the Georgia/Florida state line and perhaps even spot some wild horses on the shore as you near Cumberland Island. As the sun sets, the boat returns to Amelia Island and the music enhances the party atmosphere as the moon rises and the lights of Fernandina Beach and Center Street twinkle.

Floating down the First Coast, Jacksonville River Cruises offers public cruises on the Saint Johns River once a month. Prices start at

$45 per person and include dinner, a disc jockey and a cash bar. They offer a special cruise on Independence Day that provides a perfect vantage point for the fireworks.

For a daytime date, the St. Johns Riverkeeper organization offers monthly cruises starting at only $10. In addition to some beautiful scenery, you'll get to learn more about the delicate ecosystem of the St. Johns River. These cruises utilize the river taxis you see in operation every day in downtown Jacksonville. Different locations are featured monthly.

Amelia River Cruises 1 N. Front St Fernandina Beach 32034 www.ameliarivercruises.com (904) 261-9972

Jacksonville River Cruises 1840 Perry Place Jacksonville 32207 (904) 306-2200 www.jaxrivercruises.com

St Johns Riverkeeper (904) 256-7591 www.stjohnsriverkeeper.com 2800 University Blvd N Jacksonville 32111

Carriage Tours

What could be more romantic than a carriage ride? Some companies even offer special touches like flowers waiting for you in the carriage if you make advanced arrangements for a special occasion. If want to plan ahead, many of the carriage tour companies have websites where you can make reservations. Prices vary depending on the length of the tour as well as the privacy level: since you are aiming for romance, you want to make certain that you won't be taking a ride with loud tourists or toddlers. You can reserve a private ride for $80-$100. Communicate with your tour company about whether you desire an informative or entertaining tour versus a quiet, romantic ride. Specify your wishes; most drivers are happy to oblige. Don't forget to bring some cash for a tip. Consider taking a ride during the Nights of Lights, an annual Christmas tradition when the buildings and trees of

Saint Augustine are covered in sparkling white lights. As an added romantic touch on chilly (by Florida standards) nights, your carriage will have a blanket to snuggle under

Take a stroll down the bayfront in Saint Augustine and you'll see carriages lined up, waiting to sweep you away down historic and cobblestone streets. Historic Centre Street on Amelia Island is another perfect place to take a carriage ride. Take a romantic promenade around this Victorian seaport town and be transported back in time.

Southern Buggy Downtown St Augustine (904) 392-9952
www.southernbuggy.com

Olde Town Carriage 115 Beech St Fernadina Beach 32034
www.ameliacarriagetours.com (904) 277-1555

Ghostly Outings

Consider clutching your man's hand in fear during a chilling experience exploring paranormal oddities on Florida's oldest coast.

In Saint Augustine, the oldest city, ghostly outings abound. For exploration with a quick escape, take a ride on the Ghost Train. Board the train at the Ripley's Museum, and prepare yourself for a 90 minute tour of St Augustine's most haunted locales. This "paranormal investigation" will take you past the Castillo San Marcos, where a 1700's soldier is thought to still patrol the walls. Then the train winds past the creepy Tolomatos Cemetary to the even more disturbing French Hugenot Cemetary. Perhaps a ghostly apparition will appear, seeking peace for his soul. You'll also learn the ghostly tales of the Castle Warden building, which now houses the Ripley's Museum.

Walking ghost tours are also available in Amelia Island, where the local history is rich with tales of pirates and plunder. According to The Original Amelia Island Ghost Tour, "Paranormal activity is captured almost nightly on camera." This tour covers approximately 1.5 miles and takes a little over two hours.

If the idea of all that walking just makes you thirsty, check out Saint Augustine's Haunted Pub Hearse Ride. You, your date, and up to six others will be chauffeured around town in a gothic hearse. You will be visiting at least three haunted pubs, where you will have the opportunity to purchase a beverage (not included in the ticket price) and be regaled with tales of the eerie and paranormal. Additionally, you will visit other haunted locales including ancient cemeteries and the haunted lighthouse of Anastasia Island. Adult beverages and coolers are allowed inside the hearse as well, so this night could prove to be "one you'll wish you would have remembered." Purchase tickets online for a discounted price.

The Ghost Train 19 San Marco Ave St Augustine
www.ghosttrainadventures.com (904) 824-1606

Ghost Augustine Haunted Pub Tour/Hearse Ride (904) 814-8446
162 St George Street St Augustine www.ghostaugustine.com

The Original Amelia Island Ghost Tour 96215 Light Wind Dr
www.ameliaislandghosttours.com (904) 548-0996

Brewery Tours and Tastings

Perhaps wine isn't your thing. If you're more of a beer drinker, Jacksonville has many options. We've recently experienced a beer renaissance here on the First Coast, with some great microbreweries setting up business. However, for the traditionalists out there, I'll start at Budweiser. The Budweiser Brewery is located on the Northside of Jacksonville at 111 Busch Drive. They are open Monday through Saturday from 10 to 4 pm. Their free tour is interesting, full of history and trivia, and about 30 minutes long. At the end, you will be able to sample your top two choices of beer from their selection of nine on tap, which include ShockTop, Hoegaarden, Bud Platinum, Stella Artois and others, as well as unlimited pretzels and soda. They also offer a $25 "Beermaster" tour twice a day. The paid tour is more in-depth and includes visits to additional rooms including the control room, brewing tank room and cooling rooms (plus additional beer).

In Riverside, you will find the Intuition Ale Works and the Bold City Brewery located conveniently close to each other. The two places are quite different in atmosphere and offerings, however. Parking is iffy for both places, so you might want to try the Jax Brew Bus (www.jaxbrewbus.com or 904-352-0982). The Brew Bus will take you on a tour of 3 local craft breweries, but the cost is $50 per person.

Intuition was the first in town, located at 720 King Street (FYI, if you use the bike valet at the nearby Riverside Arts Market on Saturday mornings, you get a voucher for a free beer). You can hang out and listen to music in their modern, minimalistic tasting room. They don't serve any food here, but during peak times there are often great food trucks congregating outside. They are open from 3 to 11 Tuesday through Friday and 1 to 11pm on Saturdays. They have an open-air brewery bar when the weather is pleasant (closed June to October, when the weather is somewhat unpleasant). Brewery tours are offered by appointment only Tuesday through Friday at 3pm. Tours last 30 minutes and include a pint of beer and the glass to take home. They offer a subtle hint to tip the guide on their website: www.intuitionaleworks.com.

Bold City Brewery is located around the corner at 2670-7 Roselle Street. They offer tours on Saturday at 2pm and 5pm. They have 8 or 9 different Bold City beers on tap, and they also serve wine as well as a limited menu (burgers, brats and barbecue) prepared by Jolly Mon Catering from 4-10pm Thursday through Saturday. The Tap Room is open Thursday and Friday from 3 to 11pm and Saturday from 1 to 11pm. You can sit in the cozy tap room and play board games, foozball or even Rock'em Sock'em Robots. Now, how could that be anything but a perfect date?

Budweiser Brewery Tour 111 Busch Drive Jacksonville 32218 www.budweisertours.com (904) 696-8373

Intuition Ale Works 720 King St Jacksonville 32204 (904) 683-7720 www.intuitionaleworks.com

Bold City Brewery 2670 Roselle Street #7 Jacksonville 32204 www.boldcitybrewery.com (904) 379-6551

Jax Brew Bus www.jaxbrewbus.com (904)352-0982

Cycling

Take your sweetheart for a spin on a bike ride. Cycling together provides exercise, sunshine, and an opportunity to experience something together and interact while doing it. If you don't own bicycles, many local places offer bicycle rentals or tours.

In Amelia Island, bicycle rentals are available at Fort Clinch State Park, Pipeline Surf Shop and Beach Rentals and More. For a full map of bike paths on the island, see http://www.ameliaisland.com/uploadedfiles/bikemap.pdf. There is a 2.31 mile completed bike trail with a trail head at Little Talbot Island Park, part of the Timucuan Island Trail System. More trails are under construction or being designed. It will eventually extend north to Peters Point Park. Not far from the trailhead, you will find Kayak Amelia, which offers bike rentals as well as guided bike ecotours. Explore Fort Clinch, Fort George or Kingsley Plantation on the seat of a Trek Comfort Cruiser. The fee is $45 per person, which includes bike rental and a professional naturalist tour guide. Tours last for about two hours.

If an urban experience is what you're looking for, try Red-e to Ride in Jacksonville. They offer guided bike tours daily in Historic Riverside, Avondale, San Marco, Old Mandarin, Springfield or the Beaches. They will provide comfortable Trek bikes, or you may ride your own. Flat terrain makes it accessible to all levels of riders. Make a reservation by calling (904) 945-1571 or see www.e2ride.com Also in Jacksonville, check out the Baldwin Bike Trail, part of the "rails to trails" project. It's a 14.5 mile paved trail, with a trailhead accessible just north of interstate 10 at highway 301. In Saint Augustine, Pit Surf Shop Beach Rentals offers bicycle rentals. The shop is located adjacent to a popular beach access point, so you can take a ride along the ocean on beautiful Anastasia Island. Go at low tide to ride on packed sand.

> Fort Clinch State Park www.floridastateparks.org/fortclinch
> (904)277-7274
>
> Pipeline Surf Shop www.pipelinesurfshop.com (904) 277-3717
> 2022 1st Ave #B Fernandina Beach FL 32034
>
> Beach Rentals and More www.beachrentalsandmore.com 2021 Fletcher Ave Fernandina Beach FL 32034 (904) 310-6124
>
> Kayak Amelia www.kayakamelia.com (904)251-0016
>
> Red-e to Ride www.e2ride.com (904) 945-1571
>
> Pit Surf Shop Beach Rentals (904) 471-4700
> www.pitsurfshop.com 18 A Street St Augustine 32080

Nights of Lights

Every year from mid-November to January 31, the quaint, cobblestone streets of Saint Augustine are illuminated by the "Nights of Lights." Nights of Lights is an annual tradition in which all the buildings, the trees and bridges are all lined with twinkling white lights for the holiday season. A Light-Up Celebration takes place the Saturday before Thanksgiving in Plaza de la Constitucion, where huge trees are decked out with scores of white lights strung like pearls around a duchess' neck. The first weekend in December is a highlight of every year when the Grande Illumination takes place, featuring a candlelit march and holiday singing to mark the British period of Saint Augustine's history.

Simply taking a stroll down George Street is a magical experience at this time of year, but there are other ways to take in the lights as well. Try a romantic carriage ride for a unique way to take it all in while bundled under a carriage blanket with your sweetie. For a more raucous experience, take a ride on the Holly Jolly Trolley, and belt out Christmas carols with your fellow riders while wearing stylish 3D glasses that turn the white lights into a sparkling, multifaceted display. Make a reservation at a romantic restaurant like 95 Cordova to complete your evening, or maybe even splurge on a night at a historic inn.

Holly Jolly Trolley www.trolleytours.com (904) 829-3800
www.nightsoflights.com

[13]

Wrap it Up

"Happiness is only real when shared. " –Into the Wild (2007)

Couples Massage

If you're going to experience ecstasy, it's always better if you're not alone. Get a massage with your loved one by your side, or learn to give a massage and share the love.

Spa Laterra in Saint Augustine is a full service 9000 square foot destination day spa located in the World Golf Village. It is part of a 41-acre resort and spa community designed by noted spa architect Robert D. Henry and featured in Jacksonville Magazine. At Spa Laterra in Saint Augustine, you can rekindle the romance with a side-by-side full body massage. Floating outdoor massage cabanas are available for some services. Couples massage concludes with some alone time in a candlelit couples' retreat. After your customized massage is complete, they serve you chocolate covered strawberries to top off this romantic, rejuvenating experience. Couples massage starts at $150 for 30 minutes.

At Natural Body Spa, a couple's massage is an investment in your future, because in addition to receiving a massage, you will learn how to massage each other. What better relationship insurance can there be? Your massage therapist will teach both of you techniques for duplicating at home the healthy benefits of massage in a private room for two. Guests receive complimentary take-home massage oil and instructions. Prices start at $160 for 60 minutes. They have multiple locations; check www.naturalbody.com for one near you.

For a really special occasion, if you want to go all-out, the Ritz Carlton is naturally the way to go. They offer couples "surrender massage" in a private, romantic couple's suite. The "Couples Healing Bath and Massage" includes infrared lights to calm and soothe tensions and rich bath nutrients to fortify your skin prior to the massage. Or go for "A Wrap to Remember," which includes an aromatic soothing bath, side-by-side chocolate wrap, warm oil scalp massage and full body massage.

Spa Laterra 955 Registry Blvd St Augustine FL 32092
www.spalterra.com (904) 940-7800

Natural Body Spa www.naturalbody.com St Johns Town Center
(904) 482-0780 4663 River City Dr Jacksonville FL 32246

Ritz Carlton Amelia Island (800) 241-3333 www.ritzcarlton.com
4750 Amelia Island Pkwy Amelia Island FL 32034

[14]
Conclusion

"I don't like things that finish. One must begin something else right away." –Last Tango in Paris (1972)

It is my hope that this guide will get you out of the date night rut, provide you with some new ideas, and maybe even liven up your relationship. Here are a few final suggestions:

- Schedule a regular date night and make it a priority.
- There are 52 weeks in a year, and 50 date suggestions in this guide. You can take Thanksgiving and Christmas week off, and finish the book in one year of weekly dates.
- Keep this book in your car for last minute ideas, or have fun looking through it together to plan your next big night out.
- Take turns, alternating his and her choices.
- Make your own notes in this book so you can look back and see what you've enjoyed.
- Set a goal to try them all!
- If babysitting is a problem, try looking for solutions like taking turns with other couple friends. You can alternate weeks watching each others kids, making a bi-weekly date night possible.

- Check www.fiftyfundates.com for additions and updates to this guide.
- Call and confirm all information about businesses mentioned in this guide before heading out on your date.
- Finally, DON'T HURT YOURSELVES, PEOPLE!*

The contents of this book are for informational purposes only, and Palm Valley Press accepts no responsibility for accuracy or from any consequences resulting from use of the information in this guide. Please confirm all information directly with the businesses listed in this guide. Consult a physician before undertaking any potentially strenuous or hazardous activities.

ABOUT THE AUTHOR

Shelley Marsh lives with her husband and two sons in Ponte Vedra Beach, Florida. She is a contributing writer for Void Magazine and Shorelines.